JUST LEAD
LEADERSHIP BEGINS WITH YOU

TERRY SPAIN

JUST LEAD!!
"Leadership Begins with You"

By
Terry Spain

Let **E**verything **A**round **D**evelop

The chapters in this book are short but rich in content. This book is designed to give you strategies to help motivate you to become a better leader.

© Copyright 2020 – Terry Spain

ISBN: 978-0-578-66953-3

All rights reserved. This book is protected under the copyright laws of the United States of America. No portion of this book may be reproduced in any form without the written permission of the author.

Permission may be granted on request.

Thrive Revolution Publishing

Edited by

Cooke House Publishing

Cover designed by Troy Stubblefield

Photo taken by Ray Baldino

CONTENTS

ACKNOWLEDGMENTS 7

MY TESTIMONY 8

INTRODUCTION 10

CHAPTER 1: EDUCATE YOURSELF 11

CHAPTER 2: WHY ME? WHY NOT YOU? 12

CHAPTER 3: ACCEPT THE CHALLENGE? 13

CHAPTER 4: LEAD IN ANY COMMUNITY 14

CHAPTER 5: MY TEAM, MY SURROUNDING 15

CHAP 6: THE STREETS ARE WATCHING 16

CHAPTER 7: TAKE A RISK 17

CHAPTER 8: STICK-TO-ITIVENESS 19

CHAPTER 9: TRAVELING EQUALS A BETTER ME 21

CHAPTER 10: COMMUNICATION SKILLS AS A LEADER 23

CHAPTER 11: PICK A SHIP 24

CHAPTER 12: BUY- IN VS. COMMITMENT "THE BREAKFAST STORY" 25

CHAPTER 13: NETWORK, NETWORK, NETWORK! 26

CHAPTER 14: ARE YOU READY? 27

THE QUOTATIONS THAT HELPS MY MOTIVATION 35

NOTES 36

ABOUT THE AUTHOR 41

ACKNOWLEDGMENTS

First, I would like to thank God for allowing me and giving me the strength and fortitude to write this book. Without Him, I would be nothing. I would like to thank my lovely wife Robin Spain, for encouraging me to write this book and being there. To my awesome daughter Nia Spain, I wrote this book to show you that you can do anything you put your mind to. As you continue to grow as an adult you will be tested and encounter roadblocks, but don't let that get the best of you. You are a strong young lady who I know will do amazing things, so standby world. ☺

I have the most amazing parents in the world, and I would like to honor them by saying thank you for making me the man that I am today. It was through your leadership and guidance I am here. I was fortunate enough to have four sisters and one adopted brother. From oldest to youngest they are: Karen, Teresa, Trisha, Laura, and Trevor aka TJ. I love you and thank you for creating such wonderful nieces and nephews. ☺

To everyone who contributed to the book and encouraged me to write, thank you.

It is always great to have the love and support of family and friends, and I would like to say thank you to each of you. It's so many to name, but please know that I am thinking about you all constantly and I appreciate you for playing an active part in my life. To my hometown of Conway, South Carolina and the great people, thank you for believing in me. I would like to extend that thank you to my family in Charleston and Beaufort, SC as well.

Finally, I would like to thank all my brothers and sisters who are serving or have served this country honorably. You are the true heroes. My Prince Hall Masonic family, keep shining your light. I would like to extend a special acknowledgment to all U.S. Navy Chiefs, both retired and active duty. I may be a little bias but there is nothing like a Navy Chief. I ask that you continue to lead from the front and continue to Run the Navy. "Navy Chief Navy Pride."

MY TESTIMONY

There was a time when I used to be afraid to tell people about an event that happened in my life, but as I grew older and wiser, I realized that my story is one of triumph and not tragedy, so I decided to share and bring you into my world. This significant emotional event was a turning point in my life, and I believe it made me the person I am today.

I remember it like it happened yesterday, On July 17, 1994, I was outside playing basketball with some friends, and while playing, I started getting sharp pains in my stomach. After the final game, I went home because it was starting to throb. I went into my parents' room and told my mom that my stomach was killing me. She saw the pain I was in and she took me to the hospital. After all the routine checkups, the doctor said that it was a stomach virus going around and he believed that was the case with me.

He gave me some medicine and told me to take them, and if I don't feel any better, to come back for additional treatment. I figured since I was a strong, seventeen-year-old boy I would try to tough through the pain, and I remember going home and taking some medicine. Once I took one swallow of the pill with water, my stomach exploded, and I was immediately out. I couldn't walk and my parents immediately rushed me back to the hospital.

I remember the look on my parents and siblings' faces as they were taking me. My appendix had ruptured; I can still see the doctors' faces as they scrambled trying to save me. Quite honestly, I thought I was going to die. I said my prayers as I was being prepped for emergency surgery because I knew this was it. I had to receive two blood transfusions to help save me.

After surgery, I woke up laying in a hospital bed with family and friends looking at me. Throughout this illness, I lost almost twenty-five pounds. I had to learn how to walk all over again. I still have the marks from the tubes on my neck where I had to eat food and the scar on my stomach where I was cut. This was a lot for a seventeen-year-old kid to endure. I stayed in that hospital for one month, and during that month I had some great friends and family by my side. My friend Gerald Lawson was there every day; he also ate all my food. ☺ My friends and family motivated me daily.

I remember crying to my mom telling her, I will never be able to play basketball again or jump as high as I use to because of my scar. She would always say to me, "Yes you will, boo boo. You are going to do more than you did before." (Since we are now family, I thought I'd share my nickname.) And wouldn't you know it, she was right. So I thank God daily for her.

Who would have thought this one significant emotional event that happened in my life would have me become the person that I am today? Yes, I do realize that I could have died from this horrific moment, but I tell people all the time, I'm glad it happened. Without a test, there is no testimony. Thank you all to those that helped and encouraged me to keep striving, it's because of you I stay motivated and will continue to LEAD!

INTRODUCTION

Yes, You!

Oftentimes, we trick ourselves into not wanting to lead or take the necessary steps in becoming a great leader. Sometimes your biggest enemy is your inner self. One thing you should remember is that being a leader is not just leading in your workplace, it is also at your home and in your community. I have had the pleasure of serving in the U.S. Navy for over twenty-one years as a Chief Petty Officer. I had no choice; it was either lead from the front or get out of the way. So, once I retired, I incorporated that quote and mentality into my daily life and continued to be the leader that God has called me to be.

When I go to various events I always tell the group I am speaking to that I would like them to follow this simple direction: when I say, "Give it up," I want everyone to clap twice. Even though I am not in front of you, but you are reading this book, I want you to do the same thing: "Give it Up" (clap, clap). Doing this small gesture shows me that people can listen and they can follow directions. If by any chance the claps are off-beat or out of sync, I wait patiently until everyone gets the clapping right. As a leader, you must be in sync, and the people around you or in your circle must be the same way. This will help you in your quest to be an effective leader.

CHAPTER 1: EDUCATE YOURSELF

Education is the new currency. This is something I tell people often In my opinion, the more you know, the more you will grow. You don't have to earn a Ph.D. to be a leader, but education do go long way. Earlier in my career while serving in the Navy, education was not on the top of my list. But as I got older and wiser, I realized becoming more educated and knowledgeable wasn't so bad. I took a public speaking class earlier in my career and that prepared me to do briefings for senior officials and staff members. I started off taking one class a semester and then gradually worked my way into my Associates and later my Bachelors. This achievement has done wonders for me because I developed more confidence in myself and it shaped me into becoming the leader I am today.

I am fully aware that not everyone will take the path I did, and I also know that not everyone will go to college. But I do believe everyone should take a course that can help them on their journey to becoming a leader.

Many times, when I speak to young adults, I encourage them to look into trade schools as an option if college didn't interest them. I would later inform them that some of the wealthiest professionals are electricians, plumbers, and carpenters. After explaining to them how they can work for themselves and hire people to work for them, their attention shifts, and they become more interested. One of the key components of being a leader is developing others and encouraging people to think outside the box whether they are young or old. Education is one of my ways.

CHAPTER 2: WHY ME? WHY NOT YOU?

If I had a dollar for every time I heard someone say, *I am not cut out to be a leader like you* or *I am not a good public speaker*, I would be a millionaire. So, I would say to them, "Don't compare yourself to me, but be the best leader you can be for your family, children, and for all those who have sacrificed their lives so that you can walk the streets that you are standing in daily." "If not you, thn who?" is the saying I like to use.

Being a leader is not easy; there are long hours and a lot of sacrifices. I tell this story to people who tell me they don't want to lead. Every Thursday I teach a life skills class at the juvenile detention center, and on one Thursday, I did not want to go at all. There was a football game broadcasting on TV that I wanted to watch, and I was tired. I tried to find every excuse not to go, then this little voice in my head said get up and go, and I did just that.

I kept asking myself, *what am I going to talk to these kids about today*? I realized I had my bag where I keep a few neckties. That's when it hit me—I would teach them how to tie a necktie. Out of the fifteen (youth) that were there, not one knew how to tie a necktie. I divided them up into five groups of three and taught each one how to tie a necktie. I even taught the correctional officer.

That was one of the most powerful events as a leader for me. One of the youth said something to me that I won't ever forget. He said, "Mr. Spain, thank you for showing me how to tie a tie. I feel like I can conquer the world now." My heart dropped and I almost went into tears because I saw the look of achievement on this young man's face. He also mentioned to me that nobody in his family believed in him. These are the moments I cherish as a leader. So now ask yourself, "Why you?" And then ask yourself, "Why not you?"

CHAPTER 3: ACCEPT THE CHALLENGE?

During my time in the world's greatest Navy, I had to learn how to trust and follow. I've seen several leadership styles, some I loved and some I absolutely hated. But that groomed me to be the leader that I am right now. You ever asked yourself, How in the hell did this person become a leader? Yes, I have as well. I've also said that when I become a leader I will not lead like this person. I took mental notes and I also wrote things down that I liked in some of my leaders.

I had a leader who I worked with that used to tell me that he is following my lead and that I should take control. I used to wonder why he would put me in charge; he's the leader. I would ask him questions, questions that I knew he had the answer to, but he would make me look up the answer. Then he would have me train everyone else in the office.

I didn't like his style of leadership and thought I just wouldn't ask him for help anymore. But for some reason, I still would continue to ask for help, and once again, he would have me look it up and then train the entire office. I continue to do this for a year. After that time, he was leaving to go to another location. So, this was my opportunity to ask him why he would have me look up the answer to my question instead of just telling me the answer. His response to me was, "Spain, (in the military we call each other by last names), I am so glad you asked me that. I was waiting for you to ask me. I did that because the moment when you arrived, I immediately knew that you were a leader and had what it took to be successful. You accepted the challenge every time and I made you a better leader."

He continued by saying, "How many folks have you trained and made better by teaching important information about their careers? You learned public speaking and you learned how to research things on your own; these are all characteristics of a great leader. When I was doing the research, I didn't see it that way, but later in my career, a light bulb went off and I got it. About five years later, I called him and thanked him, and told him he made me a better person and leader. I was glad I accepted the challenge.

CHAPTER 4: LEAD IN ANY COMMUNITY

I do understand that not everyone excels in public speaking. Many shy away from the cameras or limelight but they still contribute in ways that oftentimes go unnoticed. The old saying, "there is more than one way to skin a cat" is fitting in this example that I am about to share.

I have a great friend, who doesn't make millions of dollars like athletes or prominent business owners, but he does possess something that is far greater and that is charity. His local high school basketball team needed shoes to play for the upcoming season, and without hesitation, he purchased shoes for the team. He didn't want any glory or special recognition, he simply wanted to help. On a separate occasion, he bought $5,000 in gift cards and took them to a school and said to the staff, "Anytime your students achieve something good, bless them with a gift card." I don't know about you, but as a leader that encouraged me to continue to work harder and find more ways to help the community.

I can recall a time when a gentleman came to me and said, "Terry, I need to ask you something," and I told him "Sure, go ahead." He said, "You are not even from this town. Why do you go so hard and care so much about this community and you have no ties here?" I know he didn't ask this question to be mean or rude, he just wanted to know why. At first, I was shocked, but it was a legitimate question.

I looked at him and I said, "Sir, I want to recite this quote to you and then I'll share with you my reasoning." The quote was from Mark Twain: "The two most important days in your life are the day you are born and the day you find out why." And I told him I do this because I found my why, and my why is to better any community where I live. After staring at me for about twenty seconds, He said, "Thank you for that. I need to go find my why." To me, moments like these are necessary. I had an opportunity to share with someone my purpose, and hopefully, I was able to motivate him to go out and lead and become an asset to his community.

CHAPTER 5: MY TEAM, MY SURROUNDING

I learned a long time ago that you can't do everything by yourself. As much as I tried in my younger years, it's impossible. As the old saying goes, "You are only as good as the company you keep." It is very important that you surround yourself with some solid people. I looked at Dr. Martin Luther King Jr. and the team he had around him. They were very passionate and determined individuals who joined together to achieve their visions and goals.

I am in no way the man he was, but I studied his journey, and I saw how he empowered those who were on his team. Everyone had a job to do. You couldn't be lazy or not motivated if you were on his team. So, if you as a leader are trying to lead and better this world or your community, you must have people who are willing to work and embrace their roles. If you can establish that, your goals will be that much easier to achieve. Then it will become contagious and others will see how you and the team operate and they would try to mimic that. How powerful would it be if generations embraced that concept? I use this Amish proverb often when I am out speaking on leadership or teambuilding, and I think it is fitting for this chapter: "Very few burdens are heavy if everyone lifts."

So, ask yourself these two questions:

Is my team willing and ready to lead?

_____
_____
_____
_____

If I had to pick a team of friends to help lead, who would they be?

_____
_____
_____
_____

CHAP 6: THE STREETS ARE WATCHING

I received a call from a friend which had me speechless, and for those that know me, that rarely happens. ☺ He had called me one evening and typically when we talk it's usually about sports and how his team is better than mines or vice versa. Well this call was slightly different, I will never forget it. He said, "I wanted to let you know how proud of you I am and all the work you are doing. It has not gone unnoticed and I see you and I am very honored to say I know you. You are doing an amazing job and you have inspired me." He does not know this, but that conversation brought tears to my eyes after we hung up. When I put pictures up on my social media pages, I know there are people who like your images and see the work that the team and I are doing, and from that phone call I see the effect we are having as leaders within our communities.

I often tell people when I post pictures on different social media platforms from the events I speak at, I don't post for the likes, but I post to show the world the agape love I have for the community. Anytime I see any of my friends or family doing something positive, I either email, text, or call them. Sometimes I take them out to lunch or dinner to tell them how proud I am of them. And I want you to remember, it's as equally important as a friend and leader to do the same for friends or family who are not doing positive things in the community and guide them in the right direction.

CHAPTER 7: TAKE A RISK

I know we are generally hesitant about taking risks. When I am out speaking at different events, I call up volunteers and have them line up, side by side. I can see the nervousness on some of their faces. I try to calm them down and then I explain to them and the crowd about taking a risk and that giant leap. Sometimes I just bring them up and not have them do anything but stand there and listen. I will say to them, "Many times in life, we are afraid to take the risk because we don't know what the results will be. We question will I succeed, or will I fail, and then we convince ourselves not to take the risk because we don't want to fail." I continue and talk about the product WD-40 and explain that it wasn't until the fortieth try that this product became a success. While I have their attention, I tell them to imagine if those people in that small lab in San Diego, California had given up. They would have lost out on such a dynamic and meaningful invention.

I then explain to the volunteers that are on stage with me that they will receive a reward, and I hand each of them something that they will remember this moment by whether it's a motivational bracelet, a pen or coin. And I say to them and the crowd that because they took a risk, not knowing what would happen, I reward them with a small token—all because they took a chance. I had a friend say to me, "It's your job to move people from asking to action." What I learned from that statement was we should be in the business to help those who ask and challenge them to lead.

What is your biggest fear with taking a risk?

_____

_____

_____

_____

How many times have you taken a risk and it worked or didn't work in your favor?

_____

_____

_____

_____

Did you learn from that and if so, what did you learn?

_____

_____

_____

_____

CHAPTER 8: STICK-TO-ITIVENESS

Stick-to-itiveness is a word, and according to urban dictionary, it means to stay with a project and see it through to completion. So, I think it's only fitting for leaders such as yourself to have the stick-to-itiveness to lead and remain strong in this world when it's so easy to give up and never see your dreams or vision through to completion.

For those who are parents, you may encounter times when your child wanted to give up on their homework because it's too hard or too much, and one of the first things you tell them is, you will finish this homework and I am going to check it once you are done. This concept should apply, but because you don't have the time or it's too difficult to do right now you find excuses as to why you can't complete your task. So, my question to you today is, who checking up on you. Do you have a mentor, sponsor or coach that is there to motivate you and challenge you.

I believe it's very important to have someone in your life that can help you stay the course and keep you centered. Often time, it's a friend, family member or co-worker. If I were to ask you these three questions, what would be your answer?

1. What is the one thing that I have given up on that I would love to complete?

_____

_____

_____

_____

2. Who is that person in my life that I consider my coach, mentor, or sponsor?

_____

_____

_____

_____

3. How will I apply myself as a leader to complete this task?

_____

_____

_____

_____

CHAPTER 9: TRAVELING EQUALS A BETTER ME

I've completed a lot of research on some of the world's most influential leaders and they all have mentioned how traveling to different countries has made them a better person and leader. I can attest to that and I agree with that statement 100 percent. During my travels to Africa, it gave me a new outlook on life. I felt like Patti Labelle with a new attitude. ☺

While I was in West Africa, I interacted on several occasions with the local community and worked with members of the host country military forces. I recall visiting an orphanage and seeing how those young kids were thrilled to see Americans there. One moment stood out to me and it brought tears to my eyes. There was a young girl who wanted me to adopt her and take her to the United States so she can visit New York City. She was grabbing onto my leg begging me not to leave. That that humbled me so much and one of the workers of the orphanage told me that the little girl thought I was the leader and she wanted to live with the leader.

Although I was flattered that she thought I was the leader even though my boss was standing next to me—which was humorous—but this humbled me so much because all she wanted was a better opportunity at life.

There was another time when I was in Lagos, Nigeria, and the group that I was with went to a community relations event and we were lifting 25 pounds bags of rice inside a hospital. I decided to scope out the place and see how different their hospital was in comparison to American hospital. I encountered a couple of guys who asked me was I American. When I said yes, they said simultaneously, "You are very lucky. When I inquired why, one of the gentlemen said, "Because you are rich and you have a great life and that's what we want for our children."

After explaining to them that not everyone in America is rich and living the good life, I reached into my wallet and handed them $50.00 each. I asked do they believe in God to which they both said yes. I told them to remember this scripture: "Silver and gold have none, but such as I have give thee" Acts 3:6.

I told them that it isn't money that makes you rich, it's the love in your heart for others that does. The look on their faces was priceless. I later told them that volunteering and helping in their community is worth more than the money I gave them because you will affect the lives of many people.

That moment in addition to visiting Africa was a defining moment for me as a leader. I saw people who didn't have much but they were happy. It didn't matter that some had to wash their clothes in the river and didn't care that some didn't have electricity. The one thing that they did have was love for one another. Oddly enough, six months before arriving there, I was complaining that my internet was running to slow and my light bill increased by $15.00. When I arrived back from traveling in West Africa, my entire perspective on life had changed. I began to see my purpose in life which was to lead and help others grow. So, as you are reading this chapter ask yourself these questions.

1. Where is one country that I've never visited, that I would love to go to?

_____

_____

_____

_____

2. What would you hope to get out of your trip?

_____

_____

_____

_____

3. How would you apply what you've learned as a leader to help your community?

_____

_____

_____

_____

Out of all the places you've visited, which one was your favorite? This is the question I get asked a lot. I would tell anyone who asked that Africa was the best. Then I would explain to them why, and tell them if I never visited Africa, they wouldn't be getting the Terry they know today.

CHAPTER 10: COMMUNICATION SKILLS AS A LEADER

During my time in the Navy, I was very fortunate to become a certified trainer, and one of the classes I loved to teach was Communication Skills. I use to tell my students we have so many ways to communicate, yet we are horrible at it. If you want to be a great leader, you must be a great communicator. In communication, you have the sender and the receiver. I have seen leaders become very comfortable with just sending an email thinking that would suffice. As a senior enlisted leader in the military, I had to adjust to newer communication styles from my younger personnel.

I can recall a time when one of my young Sailors was late for work; we looked all over for him. When he finally arrived at work, and I asked him why he was late, he stated that he had a doctor's appointment and had texted me on my mobile phone the previous night. I checked my phone and he indeed texted me, but I didn't see it. So, I made it a teachable moment for not only him but for the rest of the Sailors that worked for me.

I explained to them that just because you send someone a text message doesn't mean that they have seen it. I also explained that it's a good idea to call and confirm with that person if several hours have passed by and they haven't responded to your text message. I even suggested that they leave a voicemail.

I informed them I would consistently check my text and I expected them to exhaust all means of communication. After that training moment, the entire two years with them had excellent communication flow. I even learned about new communication applications, thanks to my younger Sailors. This has helped me become a better leader for sure.

CHAPTER 11: PICK A SHIP

I love to use this activity when I'm speaking at an event on leadership. I show a PowerPoint slide with two ships: one is a picture of an Aircraft Carrier which has about 5,500 personnel onboard and the other is a picture of a Destroyer which has about 250-300 personnel. I proceed to ask them if we we're going to war and the seas were rocky, which ship they would prefer to be on and why?

Most would choose the Carrier because it's big, they have planes, and it doesn't rock as much. These Sailors believed that because the Destroyer is smaller, they fear they would become seasick. Those who chose the Destroyer said they chose it because they can move around a lot quicker and they are not as big of a target.

After I listened to their explanations, I would thank them for selecting their ship, and then I would turn to the next slide and ask them, What about this ship? On the slide would be the word: leader**SHIP**. I proceed to tell them that it doesn't matter what ship you choose if you don't have great leadership, you're entire ship can suffer, and many lives could be in jeopardy.

Name one leader that has influenced you and why?

_____
_____
_____
_____
_____
_____

CHAPTER 12: BUY- IN VS. COMMITMENT
"THE BREAKFAST STORY"

There's an old fable often used in the world of business called "The Chicken and The Pig." When it comes to producing ham and eggs, you need both a chicken and a pig to contribute to the end result. However, between the two, there are distinct differences in their leadership contributions. The pig had to lay down his very life to provide the ham portion of the meal. He is more than involved in the process. He is most certainly committed to it. The chicken doesn't make nearly the same sacrifice as our dear friend, the pig. The chicken simply needs to pop out a few eggs—something that can be done on a regular basis. The chicken is involved in the meal; it's not really committed to it.

I love to tell that parable because as leaders you have to be committed, not saying you have to lay down your life, but you do have to sacrifice time and a lot of energy. But it is all worth it in the end. "The two most important abilities in a leader are avail**ability** and account**ability**." As you read this book reflect and answer these two questions.

What legacy are you leaving behind?

_____

_____

_____

_____

How committed are you as a leader?

_____

_____

_____

_____

CHAPTER 13: NETWORK, NETWORK, NETWORK!

I cannot stress this enough. There is no way of getting around it. You must network. I can honestly say I would not be where I am today if I didn't network. My friends always joke and say I know a different person in every city I travel, and if I don't, I will make one along the way. And as funny as it sounds, they are correct for the most part.

Even before the term networking became popular it has been used by people throughout this world. In order to maintain a strong relationship with other people, it's important to have good communication skills, as well as the ability to manage conflict and maintain relationships over time.

Remaining on good terms with those who have formed connections with you is key in networking. It's also very important to give as much, if not more, than you take. Sharing your connections with them will often mean they will share with you as well. Being kind is necessary and very beneficial in this scenario.

According to Forbes, "the most successful networkers build genuine relationships and give more than they receive." Rather than focusing on what you can gain, being sincere and forming real connections with people builds a real support system.

How comfortable are you with networking?

_____

_____

_____

_____

What do you hope to gain by networking?

_____

_____

_____

_____

CHAPTER 14: ARE YOU READY?

Ask yourself these series of questions:

1. How dedicated am I to lead?

_____
_____
_____
_____

2. Who was/is the most influential person or person in my life?

_____
_____
_____
_____

3. Out of all my groups of friends, which ones would I pick to give me leadership advice?

_____
_____
_____
_____

The reason why I chose these three questions is because you have to be all in. People are depending on you, and you have the potential to play a key role in someone's life. Secondly, everyone should have at least one person who influenced them the most.

The person I chose is my father, Pastor Sam T. Spain Sr, USMC Retired. The main reason I selected him is because he laid the foundation in my life so that I can be the man that I am today. And just so I won't get in any trouble, my mother did an outstanding job raising me as well—I have the best parents in the world.

Finally, I learned a long time ago, that not all your friends think like you, so once I discovered that, I had to evaluate and decipher who I can truly call friend and who is an associate. When I need marital advice, I go to my married friends. The same concept applies when I need advice about life or leadership or personal issues. I have my go-to people that I can depend on. It feels great when you know you have solid friends that you can lean on at any time. Choose wisely!

INSPIRATIONAL MESSAGES

While in the Navy, I was very fortunate enough to attain the prestigious rank of Chief Petty Officer; this rank is key and a very pivotal rank for all enlisted Sailors. There are a very small percentage of people in the Navy to obtain this rank. I would like to share some great words of encouragement given to me by some dynamic leaders that kept me going even after I retired.

1. Find two people you've led and ask them what type of leader you were to them.

2. Remember the 4 F's

First: Always be the first to set the example.

Fair: Never show Favoritism. Once you do, all respect will be lost.

Firm: Set your standard high and hold your people responsible for their actions.

Flexible: As time, people, and laws change, stay flexible and be ready to support the change.

FROM ONE LEADER TO ANOTHER: "COLLEAGUES PERSPECTIVES"

As a leader, I most certainly value the knowledge and wisdom of other leaders. I asked these four great leaders to contribute to this book and without hesitation they accepted the request.

"PERSPECTIVE ON LEADERSHIP" - MR. GARY RICHARDSON

Over the past 30 years, I've had the opportunity of experiencing leadership from the perspectives of both a subordinate and a leader. During both my careers as a New York State Trooper and member of the United States Air Force, I rose through the ranks starting out as a road trooper with the New York State Police and being promoted to the ranks of Sergeant, Station Commander, and then Technical Lieutenant in charge of the Equal Employment Opportunity Compliance Office.

In the Air Force, I began my career as an enlisted member with the rank of E-3 and ended my career as a Major, in which I was assigned as the Program Manager of the Senior Leadership Training Branch for the Department of Defense. These experiences allowed me to see, feel, and hear leadership from a dual perspective, one as a follower and the other as someone responsible for leading others. I found that leadership is as dynamic as those who are selected to administer it and the circumstances under which they must perform their duties serve as a test of their abilities to be successful at it.

Therefore, my perspective on leadership is that one must be welled versed on two things: human relations (not as a profession, but in the way humans relate with each other) and persuasion, the ability to get others to do what it is a leader needs them to do. Leadership is about guiding people to meet the requirements of the organization during a moment in time. Because a leader cannot always anticipate what will happen on any given day, he or she must employ the experiences and skill sets of employees and subordinates to accomplish their tasks.

The more a leader knows and understands how the people he or she is leading will act and respond under certain conditions will help them reach the desired outcome the organization is seeking.

This requires getting to know the individual employee on a much deeper level then simply knowing their names and what they do for the company. Great leadership requires trust in the leader and being made to feel valued by him or her.

Even when the organization is not well regarded as a whole, in my experience it has been witnessed that subordinates will still support leaders they trust and believe in. It's this trust that will make it easier to persuade others to do what needs to be done. It must be remembered that leadership is always about guiding people to a desired outcome. Although leaders are often required to manage as well, people aren't the objects of management, their skill sets are. Employees must comply with orders and taskings, but they don't have to be fully committed to their jobs or the organization. I wanted employee commitment, so I adapted my leadership style with this in mind to get it.

I've stood by this principle throughout my careers as a leader. It wasn't a magic solution and there were still challenges I faced daily. However, all the awards and accolades I've received during my careers are an indication that this philosophy was effective. Those I led performed their duties exceptionally well and supported my vision as a leader. Their efforts were recognized and rewarded, and as their leader mine were too.

WHAT DOES BEING A LEADER MEAN TO ME? - MR. RAY KEMP

In Navy boot camp 1986, I was told by the Company Commander (aka Drill Instructor) "Leadership is the art of influencing people to execute a mission that may cost them their lives. A good leader will get his men to go into a fight with a smile and a snarl knowing they shall be victorious!"

That was the day I was assigned as the SIXTH Squad leader and I led Sailors for the next 33 years. As time moved, on my personal definition of leadership evolved based on experience, assignments, education, culture, and maturity. To me, being a leader means that you have the honor of being accountable and responsible for the most precious asset of any organization, the people who will execute an action that is self-defined or defined by the organization. Depending on that task at hand, there are many factors that determine the style of leadership that is applied to motivate a team to action.

No matter the task, education of the group, or criticality to the organization, the need for precision communications and approachability/charisma is necessary for high level accomplishment. Approachability/charisma is crucial to feedback-rich environments which genuinely seek the most efficient and effective solutions through questioning attitudes and loyalty.

In summation, being a leader is an opportunity to have a positive impact on hearts and minds, develop critical thinking, and complete assigned tasks at a level that makes the individual team members proud to be part of an organization.

WHAT DOES BEING A LEADER MEAN TO ME?

Leadership is the art of influencing people to selflessly execute a mission/assignment to their fullest capability while empowered to provide feedback on how to do it better.

LEADERSHIP - MR. GREGORY TYRONE COLE

The best leaders have the ability to communicate effectively and build honest relationships while inspiring those who follow. The fundamental elements of our society require a leadership structure.

Basically, this fact requires that there are leaders in our everyday lives, whether by title or action. I prefer to think that true leadership is fully shown through actions rather than position or title. While a president holds a large amount of power to leads others, a mother, father, or coach are oftentimes better leaders through their positive actions and ability to inspire others.

To me, true leadership is best displayed by the courageous actions of those that lead by good example and inspire others to follow that good example.

There are of course bad leaders, but those that do not set a good example and inspire others, rarely stay leaders for long.

When I think of leadership examples in my life, I think of people I have encountered that bring out the best in those they lead. Every good leader should have elements of confidence and humility. I have rarely seen a person who enjoys following someone who lacks confidence, but even more so, most people really dislike a leader who is so overconfident to the point that they are condescending or lacking in humility.

True leadership requires an individual to be authentic and sincere. Most people can overlook a leader's mistake if they truly show remorse and can honestly communicate that remorse with their followers. Today, more than ever, we need trustworthy leaders who build and sustain relationships through effective, sincere, and inspiring communication. After all, who wants to follow a leader they can't trust? Not me.

> "IT'S NOT HOW MANY PEOPLE YOU LEAD, BUT IT'S HOW MANY PEOPLE YOU MAKE LEADERS!"
>
> –GREGORY TYRONE COLE

WHAT DOES BEING A LEADER MEAN TO YOU? - MR. EDWARD JOHNSON

Although many may share similar leadership traits, no leader is the exact same. As much as all would love to be that great leader and go-to person, it is important to understand your calling and your timing for your specific assignment, so that your leadership capabilities will best benefit the organization. You may talk to ten different leaders and get ten different explanations of what being a leader means. Many may share similar beliefs and values, but there is no definitive answer on exactly what it means to be a leader.

Many are placed in leadership positions, but not all have the ability to be an effective leader. A leader can be coached or mentored to be effective, which is necessary for any organization to produce a desired or intended result for its mission. However, I believe that great leaders are naturally chosen from birth with the ability to lead. If you visit a day care or playground and watch children interact with each other, you will always see the few that stand out amongst the rest.

You will see toddlers following other toddlers. Those leading will generally continue to be stand out leaders. Combine the natural calling on their life to lead with personal experiences, to include accomplishments, failures, victories, let downs, acceptance, traumas, will, insecurities, favor, loneliness, determination, quitting, transparency, denial, morals, and character, and now you have a great recipe for what I consider a great leader.

The most important piece of information to know when leading is your mission and purpose. Without knowing this it is very difficult to reach any kind of goal or make a difference in anyone's life or organization. When I served in the military, we had a saying, "Lead, Follow, or Get out of the Way." A very important component of leading is having the ability to adapt. Sometimes it is your moment to lead and other times it is necessary for you to follow. Every leader must be a great follower.

Just because you are an effective leader or great leader does not mean you have to be the person to lead all the time. Part of being an effective leader means knowing your strengths and areas of improvement and when to step aside or empower others to best benefit the goal set forth. One may let pride dictate their emotions to feel like they are less competent than the next person, when in reality having the ability to do this makes you that much more of an effective leader and asset to your organization.

It is very important to be able to regulate your time, attention and emotions, while remaining aware of your strengths, weaknesses, and potential sources of bias. In order to be an effective leader, you must be an effective follower. Some of the goals I set for myself when leading is being that person that inspires and motivates people to be the best possible form of THEMSELVES!

In the quest to achieve that, I practice setting and being the example for others to emulate and follow. I pride myself on being humble, truthful, transparent, and of good moral standing. I ensure that I treat everyone with respect, from the teenager on their first day as part of the organization all the way up to the senior person that's been there for thirty years.

I practice taking ownership of my actions and the actions of those I am leading while holding them accountable, but also letting them know that I am not perfect and have made similar mistakes and had to face the consequences. I work hard at having the ability to motivate people to achieve a common goal based on building a relationship on trust and loyalty rather than fear or positional power.

A true effective leader must be close enough to relate to others, but far enough ahead to motivate them. In closing, never forget where you came from. Never forget those emotions, frustrations, and struggles when in previous positions. By doing this, you are able to be transparent, relatable, and approachable, which all leads to successful leaders, successful subordinates, successful organization, successful goals, and a successful life.

THE QUOTATIONS THAT HELPS MY MOTIVATION

I love reading quotes that inspire me on a daily basis. I have compiled a series of quotes that I use either when I'm speaking or just for daily encouragement. I hope as you read these quotes it will encourage you as much as they do for me.

- "Dedicate yourself to a core set of values. Without them, you will never be able to find personal fulfillment, and you will never be able to lead effectively." — Kenneth Chenault

- "I never lose, I either win or learn." —Nelson Mandela

- "Don't ever wrestle with a pig; you both will get dirty but the pig will enjoy it." —Cale Yarborough

- "It's fine to celebrate success but it is more important to heed the lessons of failure." – Bill Gates, co-founder of Microsoft

- "Some people want it to happen, some wish it would happen, others make it happen." – Michael Jordan, Hall of Fame basketball superstar

- "Success isn't about how much money you make; it's about the difference you make in people's lives." — Michelle Obama

- "Have a vision. Be demanding."– Colin Powell

- "The pessimist complains about the wind. The optimist expects it to change. The leader adjusts the sails." —John Maxwell

- "I have nothing in common with lazy people who blame others for their lack of success. Great things come from hard work and perseverance. No excuses. -Kobe Bryant

- "One small crack does not mean that you are broken. It means that you were put to the test and you did not fall apart." - Linda Poindexter.

- "Don't enable people, help people become able."- Terry Spain

NOTES

NOTES

NOTES

NOTES

NOTES

ABOUT THE AUTHOR

Terry Spain a native of Conway, S.C. is the CEO of Terry Spain Consulting LLC, which specializes in diversity and leadership training along with motivational speaking and team building. Before retiring from the U.S Navy, Terry served as the Senior Instructor for the Senior Leadership Development Branch and Lead Navy Facilitator at the Defense Equal Opportunity Management Institute (DEOMI). He has trained members of the Federal Government, the White House, Camp David, and the Naval Academy.

Terry holds a host of credentials to include Organizational Management, Department of Defense Certified Mediator, Certified Small Group Facilitator, Diversity Trainer, Command Climate Specialist, EEO Counselor, Certified Workshop Facilitator, and Certified Facilitator Evaluator/Trainer.

As a pillar in the community, he is an active member of the NAACP Central Brevard Branch and serves as the Veterans committee Chairman. Terry is also member of the Brevard County Chamber of Commerce (Military Affairs Council) and serves as an advisor for the Bob Feller Act of Valor Foundation. Additionally, he volunteers as a mentor to young males and teaches a life skills course at the Brevard Regional Juvenile Center in Cocoa, Fl. He also serves as a mentor and trainer for INROADS.

Mr. Spain received his Bachelor's degree from Thomas Edison state university in Trenton, NJ and his Certificate of Mastery in Diversity & Inclusion from The Institute for Federal Leadership in Diversity & Inclusion (Georgetown University). He has served over 21 years in the U.S. Navy and attained the rank of Chief Petty Officer. As a veteran of the United States Navy, Terry was assigned to various ships and bases around the world, which allowed him to gain in-depth life experiences relating to diversity and leadership.

In 2014, Terry was awarded The National Association for the Advancement of Colored People (NAACP) Roy Wilkins Renown Service Award.

www.ingramcontent.com/pod-product-compliance
Lightning Source LLC
Chambersburg PA
CBHW070304010526
44108CB00039B/1857